W9-AKD-573

A BLUE BANNER
BIOGRAPHY

Allen Iverson

Wayne Wilson

P.O. Box 196
Hockessin, Delaware 19707
Visit us on the web: www.mitchelllane.com
Comments? email us: mitchelllane@mitchelllane.com

Mitchell Lane PUBLISHERS

Copyright © 2005 by Mitchell Lane Publishers. All rights reserved. Updated August 2006. No part of this book may be reproduced without written permission from the publisher. Printed and bound in the United States of America.

Printing   3   4   5   6   7   8   9

Blue Banner Biographies

Alicia Keys	**Allen Iverson**	Alan Jackson
Ashanti	Ashlee Simpson	Ashton Kutcher
Avril Lavigne	Bernie Mac	Beyoncé
Bow Wow	Britney Spears	Christina Aguilera
Christopher Paul Curtis	Clay Aiken	Condoleezza Rice
Daniel Radcliffe	Derek Jeter	Eminem
Eve	50 Cent	Gwen Stefani
Ice Cube	Jamie Foxx	Ja Rule
Jay-Z	Jennifer Lopez	J. K. Rowling
Jodie Foster	Justin Berfield	Kate Hudson
Kelly Clarkson	Kenny Chesney	Lance Armstrong
Lindsay Lohan	Mariah Carey	Mario
Mary-Kate and Ashley Olsen	Melissa Gilbert	Michael Jackson
Miguel Tejada	Missy Elliott	Nelly
Orlando Bloom	Paris Hilton	P. Diddy
Peyton Manning	Queen Latifah	Rita Williams-Garcia
Ritchie Valens	Ron Howard	Rudy Giuliani
Sally Field	Selena	Shirley Temple
Tim McGraw	Usher	

Library of Congress Cataloging-in-Publication Data
Wilson, Wayne, 1953–
    Allen Iverson / Wayne Wilson.
       p. cm. — (A blue banner biography)
    Includes bibliographical references and index.
    ISBN 1-58415-328-8 (lib. bdg.)
    1. Iverson, Allen, 1975– 2. Basketball players—United States—Biography—Juvenile literature.
I. Title. II. Series.
GV884.I84W55 2005
796.323'092—dc22

2004021874

ISBN-10: 1-58415-328-8   ISBN-13: 9781584153283

ABOUT THE AUTHOR: Wayne Wilson was born and raised in Los Angeles. He received a Master of Arts in Education from the University of California, Los Angeles. For 16 years he was co-owner and president of a pioneering and innovative publishing company specializing in multicultural designs. He's completed interviews with influential Latino men throughout the country and has written over 160 biographies for *Encuentros: Hombre A Hombre*, a comprehensive vocational education book to be published in commercial and literary magazines. Wilson lives in Venice Beach, California, with his wife and daughter and has recently had his first screenplay, *The Deal*, optioned.

PHOTO CREDITS: Cover—Barry Gossage/NBAE/Getty Images; p. 4—Pablo Martinez Monsivais/AP Photo; p. 6—George Widman/AP Photo; p. 10—Joe Murphy/NBAE/Getty Images; p. 13—Routers; p. 16—AP Photo/Daily Press, Jane Hwang; p. 20—Doug Mills/AP Photo; p. 23—Chuck Burton/AP Photo; p. 25—Andrew Cohoon/AP Photo; p. 28—AFP Photo/Mike Nelson; p. 29—Michael Conroy/AP Photo.

PUBLISHER'S NOTE: The following story has been thoroughly researched, and to the best of our knowledge, represents a true story. While every possible effort has been made to ensure accuracy, the publisher will not assume liability for damages caused by inaccuracies in the data, and makes no warranty on the accuracy of the information contained herein. This story has not been authorized nor endorsed by Allen Iverson.

CONTENTS

Allen Iverson holds his Most Valuable Player trophy at the end of the 50th NBA All-Star Game at the MCI Center in Washington on February 11, 2001. He scored 25 points in the 111-110 win over the Western Conference.

The Answer

*I*n 1996, Allen Iverson became the smallest first-overall draft pick in the history of the National Basketball Association. He was selected by the Philadelphia 76ers in the hope that the point guard would be a franchise player and revitalize the ailing team. Before he played his first professional game, Iverson proclaimed himself—both verbally and by a tattoo printed on his left arm—The Answer. Ironically, the nickname seemed to usher in more questions than answers when he was signed by the 76ers, who list him at 6 feet tall and 165 pounds, although many argue he is closer to 5 feet 10 inches and weighs less.

But the first question, could Allen Iverson play in the NBA's land of big men, was immediately answered during his debut game of the 1996–97 NBA season when he scored 30 points in an opening-night loss to the Milwaukee Bucks. With his explosive and mesmerizing

In May of 1999, during an overtime game against the Detroit Pistons, Iverson staked his claim to the scoring title being the first 76er to win since Wilt Chamberlain.

style of "street ball," Iverson not only earned rookie of the month honors for November and April, but he also became the first rookie to score 40 points or more in five consecutive games, breaking the previous record of three games set by Hall of Fame center Wilt Chamberlain during the 1959–60 season. Iverson, whose crossover dribble has been heralded as the best in basketball, says a lot of his moves were created on the playgrounds.

Despite his small frame, Iverson has a 44-inch vertical leap and a seven-foot wingspan. "His speed is blinding and sometimes you get caught up in watching him go," says teammate Aaron McKie.

During his first pro season, Iverson compiled an impressive list of statistics, including winning both NBA Rookie of the Year and MVP in the Rookie All-Star Game. But despite his amazing quickness and the excitement he brought to the game, the 76ers ended the 1996–97 season with a dismal 22–60 record, the fifth worst in the league. Furthermore, Iverson led the NBA in turnovers as a rookie and was criticized for being a selfish star who appeared more interested in personal statistics than team accomplishments. After an early-season game against the Chicago Bulls, NBA legend Michael Jordan stated the trash-talking rookie needed to show him more respect. "I wasn't trying to disrespect the best player ever," Iverson defends, "but when you're on the court, you can fear no one. Do that, you lose your game."

> *Despite his small frame, Iverson has a 44-inch vertical leap and a seven-foot wingspan. "His speed is blinding . . ."*

Little Big Man

L ove him or hate him, Iverson's fearlessness is the very reason he has been so successful in his NBA career. With his blinding speed, deadly crossover dribble, excellent jump shot, and ability to withstand the pounding he takes every night from NBA defenders, Iverson commands new respect with each performance.

In summer 2001 Iverson had surgery to remove bone spurs. He found the rehabilitation period particularly trying as he waited for doctors to say he could play again. "Just getting back on the court, I feel like a kid in a candy store," remarked Iverson. He hates missing games and dislikes resting so much that—as his coach Larry Brown knows—even in a blowout, it's easier just to leave him in the game than to try to convince him to take a break.

When he returned to the court, the smallish superstar led the 76ers to their first Eastern Conference championship in nearly two decades and ultimately to the NBA Finals, where they were defeated by the Los Angeles Lakers. For his efforts Iverson not only won the 2001 scoring title and the All-Star MVP trophy, but he was voted by a national panel of sportswriters and broadcasters as the NBA's Most Valuable Player.

According to the *Chicago Tribune*, Iverson was the only player named on every ballot and the first player since Michael Jordan in 1993 to lead the league in scoring and steals. The award is usually given to the person generally considered the NBA's most dominant player. Iverson gained the distinction of being the smallest and lightest player to be named MVP.

When asked about his tenacity and willingness to keep getting up after being knocked down, Iverson says: "I did not give up when a lot of people I've seen in my life give up. I felt I owed too much to my kids, my wife, my family and friends, all the people who have been with me through the struggles in my life."

> "I did not give up when a lot of people I've seen in my life give up. I felt I owed too much to my kids, my wife, my family and friends . . ."

During the 2001 playoffs Iverson showed he could be as tough as they come, boldly driving the lane and scoring on opponents who are a foot taller and 100 pounds heavier. At times he seemed to score virtually at will. In the first game of the NBA Finals, Iverson torched the Los Angeles Lakers for 48 points, handing them their only playoff loss and causing Laker Robert Horry, one of the team's best defenders, to question whether anyone could stop the dynamic guard. He told *Time*, "He can get the jumper anytime he wants, so all you can do is hope he's not hitting it. If he drives, you have to hope the help comes quick enough. There's a lot of hope involved."

Iverson has sometimes been criticized for being too arrogant.

Sandy Banks, columnist for the *Los Angeles Times*, claims Allen Iverson's appeal during the playoffs was simple: "We like to root for the underdog. He was the tiniest, toughest man on the court, leading a crew of injury-plagued teammates through valiant battle against the game's most talented team."

Rapping to His Own Beat

*I*verson's popularity has grown tremendously due to his extraordinary skills and mental toughness. On the other hand, he also has a fair number of critics. Controversy has constantly swirled around the young superstar. Iverson has been criticized by the press and veteran players for what is sometimes perceived as arrogance. His wild, partying lifestyle, his hair stitched in elaborate cornrows, and the way he dresses have been subjects of intense scrutiny. Some maintain that he glorifies the "gangsta" image, with his tough entourage and twenty-one tattoos, diamond-studded jewelry and gold chains, baggy jeans, and do-rags.

"I don't worry about impressing anyone," contends Iverson. "The people who count to me are my family and my friends. . . . I didn't come here worried about anything anyone was going to say. I knew I was Iverson, the number one draft choice, with a big bull's-eye painted on my back."

Despite his six-year, $70.9 million 76ers contract and 10-year, $50 million Reebok deal, Iverson says that still, "people attack everything I do." Not only is he a basketball star and a talented [artist], he has tried his hand as a rapper, under the name Jewelz. He began the 2000–2001 season awash in controversy over the obscene lyrics in his rap CD, *Non-Fiction*. A furor was created when *The Philadelphia Inquirer* printed the lyrics to one single, "40 Bars," which depicts women as objects and makes fun of homosexuals. Consequently, women's and gay groups protested the release of the single. The album also distressed organizations ranging from the NBA to the NAACP, leading to a meeting with NBA commissioner David Stern.

> **Not only is he a basketball star and a talented [artist], he has tried his hand as a rapper, under the name Jewelz.**

As Iverson told *Sports Illustrated*, "People who are into rap know what I'm talking about. . . . If I was trying to make everyone happy, I could only rap about cartoons and The Rugrats. My hip-hop fans wouldn't accept that."

Originally the album was scheduled to come out during the February 2001 All-Star break, but due to the controversy over some of the lyrics in his songs, the release was delayed until 2002. Despite the conflict over his music, Iverson has still won the praise of many critics in the past years for his heroic feats on the basketball court.

But Allen Iverson has always rapped to his own beat. This is the same man who also wears a "What Would Jesus Do?" bracelet strapped around an arm covered with tattoos, and who affectionately kissed his six-year-old daughter during halftime of the championship game.

Iverson holds his 2001 Most Valuable Player Trophy with pride.

Birth of a Superstar

On June 7, 1975, Allen Ezail Iverson was born to Ann Iverson in Hampton, Virginia. At the time she was fifteen years old and unmarried. According to *Sports Illustrated*, Iverson's father, Allen Broughton, was a point guard and the leader of a gang called the Family Connection. According to published reports, Iverson barely knows his biological father.

Ann Iverson is an avid basketball fan. She is often seen at her son's games wearing expensive jewelry and a mink hat and mink coat over a custom-made "Iverson's Mom" number 3 jersey. She recalled in the same 2001 *Sports Illustrated* interview that she was still playing basketball when she was five months pregnant with Allen. It wasn't until she got into a fight with another girl while pregnant that her grandmother decided it was time to move the family from Connecticut to Hampton, Virginia, where Allen was born.

"When the nurse brought him to me," Ann Iverson recalls, "I looked at his little body and saw these long arms and said, 'Lord, he's gonna be a basketball player!'" Allen was nicknamed after his uncles, Bubba and Chuck, and known around family and friends as Bubbachuck. To support her family, which also included Allen's two sisters, Ann Iverson worked a variety of jobs, including a secretary at Langley Air Force Base, a welder at the shipyard, and an Amway salesperson.

It was Ann Iverson who got Allen involved in sports at a young age. She signed him up for a youth basketball league—much to Allen's chagrin, because his first love was football. Allen Iverson recounts: "I didn't want to try it, I thought basketball was a stupid sport. I cried all the way out the door when she sent me to basketball practice. But I played and I liked it."

At Bethel High School in Virginia, Iverson was a starter in both football and basketball. During the summers he played basketball in a special league with some of the best high school players in the country. Coached by Boo Williams, a former St. Joseph player, his team won the National Amateur Athletic Union tournament, and Iverson was named MVP in five other tournaments. He was also

"I didn't want to try it, I thought basketball was a stupid sport. I cried all the way out the door when she sent me to basketball practice. But I played and I liked it."

Iverson visits the Boys and Girls Club in Newport News, Virginia.

phenomenal in football. He quarterbacked the team to the state championship and was named Virginia's high school football player of the year.

The only thing at which Iverson did not excel was academics, and he frequently skipped school. The class he showed the most interest in was art. Fortunately his athletic skills offered him a great deal of national attention, and he was sure to receive a college scholarship.

A Troubled Life

*C*ontroversy accompanied Allen Iverson before he ever stepped onto an NBA court. During his senior year of high school, on February 13, 1993, Iverson and a group of friends went bowling in Hampton, Virginia. Reportedly, when they went to order food, their behavior was rowdy and management asked them to quiet down. A group of white males in their 20s was seated there, and supposedly the word "nigger" was uttered. A brawl ensued between the parties. Allegedly Iverson was in the middle of it, although he maintains that he did not hit anyone. He and three other black men were arrested. This was not the first time Iverson had run afoul of the law: He had been assigned to a probation officer after being caught twice driving without a license.

In July 1993 Iverson was convicted of maiming by mob and was sentenced to 15 years in jail, 10 of them suspended. This created an uproar in the community, and many critics argued that the harshness of the sentence was comparable to ones given for rape and manslaughter. Plus, the fact that no whites were charged led to racial tensions in the area, which culminated in protest marches and "Free Iverson" T-shirts.

Iverson began serving his sentence at the Newport News City Farm, a minimum-security facility near Hampton, in September 1993. While in prison, Iverson worked in the facility's bakery and studied with a tutor in an effort to keep up with his schoolwork. He served four months in prison, and as his appeals were pending, he was granted conditional clemency by Virginia governor Douglas Wilder. His conviction was overturned completely in June 1995. "I wear a gold necklace in the shape of handcuffs to remind me of where I never want to go back," said Iverson.

"I wear a gold necklace in the shape of handcuffs to remind me of where I never want to go back," said Iverson.

While it appeared that Allen's dreams of playing basketball and football were rapidly disappearing, Ann Iverson met with John Thompson, the coach of the Georgetown Hoyas. Thompson was known for his tough-love approach and had nurtured such basketball stars as Patrick Ewing and Alonzo Mourning. He was also one of the first African-American coaches to work at a predominantly white university. Despite the criticisms he would endure for bringing a poor black student with a troubled past to an elite academic institution, Thompson gave Iverson the opportunity to right his career. He admits, however, that after several initial meetings with Iverson, if he hadn't seen some commitment and a willingness to succeed on Iverson's part, he never would have gotten involved.

Encouraged by Thompson's faith in him, Iverson attended Richard Milburn High School in Virginia Beach. The private school was for at-risk youths. While there, Iverson earned his last high school credit and received his diploma. He also scored well enough on the SAT to qualify to play for Georgetown in the fall of 1994.

In his first exhibition game at Georgetown against an Army team from Fort Hood, Iverson scored 24 points in the first seven minutes. He impressed even skeptical spectators, who yelled "Jailbird" while he was at the free-throw line.

During his first year at Georgetown, Iverson made the typical mistakes of many young players: trying to do too much himself, and not always being aware of his teammates. Thompson's method of coaching Iverson was

> *In his first exhibition game at Georgetown against an Army team from Fort Hood, Iverson scored 24 points in the first seven minutes.*

Iverson receives a pat on the head from his teammate Victor Page during Georgetown's 73-62 victory over New Mexico during round two NCAA play on March 17, 1996 at the Richmond Coliseum in Virginia. Iverson scored 19 points in the second half.

to try to strike a balance between instilling discipline and allowing Allen the freedom to play in his lightning-speed, flashy style.

"He taught me a lot of things: how to deal with people, how to deal with different situations, and always think 'life' before anything," says Iverson about Coach

Thompson. Iverson averaged 23 points, 4.6 assists, and 3.2 steals per game over his two seasons at Georgetown. In his sophomore year he led the Hoyas to a 29–8 record and the Eastern Regional Finals. He also managed to earn respectable grades and considered majoring in English or fine arts. However, after two years, at the age of 20, Iverson decided to enter the NBA draft.

In 1997, after having a sensational first season in the NBA and being named the NBA's Rookie of the Year, Iverson was arrested again. He had been a passenger in a speeding Mercedes stopped by Virginia police. An officer found a Glock Model 21 handgun under Iverson's seat and a marijuana cigarette on it. The charges were dropped after Iverson completed 100 hours of community service. In 1998, Iverson's bodyguard was charged with assault and rape. Subsequently two of Iverson's friends, who were driving Iverson's car, were arrested and charged with drug possession.

One of the reasons Iverson gets into trouble is that unlike many pro athletes, who run away from all reminders of their past, Iverson is in no rush to sever ties with his. He believes in "keeping it real." He is intensely

> *In 1997, after having a sensational first season in the NBA and being named the NBA's Rookie of the Year, Iverson was arrested again.*

loyal to his childhood pals from the projects in Hampton. "My friends are me. These guys have been with me since I was a kid and were always down for me. . . . We're being criticized because we're young black men who dress a certain way, talk a certain way and are hip-hop—not preppy and not what people want to see."

> *He believes in "keeping it real." He is intensely loyal to his childhood pals from the projects in Hampton. "My friends are me. . . ."*

"I wouldn't dare try to tell him to abandon the people who are a part of his life," says 76ers coach Larry Brown. "But he's in a different position than his friends. Kids wear his shoes and shirts and look up to him."

One NBA veteran described the relationship between Larry Brown and Allen Iverson as the worst relationship between coach and star player he's ever witnessed. The tension between the two individuals weighed on everyone. Brown almost quit before the 2000–2001 season, claiming he was not going to endure another year trying to coach "someone who takes any criticism as a personal attack." Many of Iverson's teammates were also dissatisfied with Iverson's antics and sided with Brown. They had grown tired of Iverson's blaming his irresponsibility on childhood hardships, extreme poverty, and having a father and stepfather in

Head coach Larry Brown directs the 76ers in the fourth quarter of their 92-82 win at the Charlotte Coliseum in Charlotte, NC, on April 22, 2000 during the first round of the NBA playoffs.

prison. One anonymous teammate said, "Half the 'brothers' grew up in so-called 'hard lives' and we're doing what we're supposed to."

Teammate Aaron McKie tried to help steer Allen straight. He too grew up without a father, and his family lived for a time in a car. "I'd probably have jumped off a bridge if I had his pressures. But I tell him that being late and fussing with the coach doesn't help matters at all. That's gotta go!"

Challenge and Commitment

*T*hings had gotten so bad that, fearing Iverson was becoming uncontrollable, the 76ers attempted to trade him during the summer of 2000, but Iverson managed to convince team president Pat Croce that he should remain in Philadelphia. Croce mediated an uneasy truce between Iverson and Brown, but the brunt of the agreement rested on Iverson's shoulders. He was told to follow the coach's rules and regulations or he was going to be traded. Iverson accepted the challenge.

In an interview with Sam Smith of the *Chicago Tribune*, he said: "A lot of things happened between myself and coach Brown, and some nights I had to go home and look in the mirror at some of the things I was doing and they were not right. All the baggage I came in with. I was 21 years old. Everyone wanted Allen Iverson to be 30 years old. Nobody gave me space for error. Everybody wanted me to be a veteran because of the

Iverson goes up for a shot over New Orleans Hornets' David Welsey in the first half of the game at New Orleans Arena on March 17, 2004.

talent God gave me. It took some time, I kept fighting. I worked on things people said I couldn't do."

Iverson sought to take responsibility for his life. The first thing he did was ask Coach Brown to appoint him team co-captain, and the coach agreed. Iverson figured if he was going to talk the talk about changing his ways, he wanted to walk the walk, too. About the controversy regarding his CD, he issued an apology and also met with civil rights groups and gay and lesbian leaders. In the 2000–2001 season he missed just two games, despite a flurry of injuries he suffered during the year. He was late for only one practice and called to let the organization know.

"I finally looked in the mirror," Iverson reiterated. "This is my fifth year, and I haven't won a championship.

I had to stop acting like a kid and start doing some extra work. There were a lot of small things Coach Brown wanted me to do that I didn't do and should've never had a problem doing. Now I'm doing them." Iverson made a more concerted effort to get his teammates involved in the game, hitting them for the open shot when he was double- and triple-teamed instead of always trying to make the highlight film for the national news. As a result he was able to take his team to the NBA Finals and was named MVP for the league.

As a sign of overcoming his "bad boy" image, Iverson established the Allen Iverson Summer Classic Foundation and the Crossover Foundation.

As a sign of overcoming his "bad boy" image, Iverson established the Allen Iverson Summer Classic Foundation (AISCF) and the Crossover Foundation. These organizations were created to help inner-city youths with their transition to adulthood and to help them become productive members of society. The Crossover Foundation encourages kids to stay in school and to avoid drugs, teen pregnancy, and gang activity. Last year, the AISCF also created the Allen Iverson Relief Fund to provide immediate relief to families who were victims of the September 11 terrorist attacks.

Also, in the winter of 2001, Iverson signed a lifetime endorsement and marketing contract with Reebok, an extension of the deal the star signed in 1996 after being selected the number one overall pick in the NBA draft. "Allen's love for the game is clearly demonstrated each time he takes the court," said Paul Fireman, chairman and chief executive officer of Reebok International Ltd.

"It shows a lot of commitment, and hopefully I can stand up to my part," Iverson said. "I didn't have the greatest past in the world, but they always stood by me and always stood up for me when times were bad."

When he was presented the 2001 All-Star MVP trophy, he wanted to share the spotlight with Larry Brown. He asked, "Where's my coach?"

Coach Brown remarked, "It was one of the proudest moments of my career. I just want the kid to develop as a human being and as possibly the best player ever in this league."

> *For all the turmoil around Allen Iverson, those who know him insist that behind his defiant swagger is a decent young man with a good heart.*

For all the turmoil around Allen Iverson, those who know him insist that behind his defiant swagger is a decent young man with a good heart. Even Coach Brown describes him as "a good family man" with his two kids, Tiaura and "Deuce" (Allen II), by his longtime girlfriend, Tawanna Turner. In August 2001, in a celebrity-filled ceremony at the Mansion in Voorhees Township in

Iverson with his children Deuce (Allen II) and Tiaura.

southern New Jersey, Allen and Tawanna were finally married.

Johnny Davis, Iverson's coach during his rookie season with Philadelphia and now an Orlando assistant, says about Iverson, "He's always been a likable guy. . . . And I think the image or the reputation he got early in his career wasn't deserved. I feel that if people really knew who Allen Iverson was, they would understand that this is not a bad young man."

John Thompson adds, "People try to define superstars with sound bites out of their lives. That's the unfortunate part of sports. You don't have the opportunity to know people enough before passing judgment. Allen is a pretty special person, in my opinion."

In 2004, Allen was privileged to represent the United States in the Summer Olympics in Athens, Greece. Though the U.S. was only able to walk away with a

Allen Iverson smiles during a 77-71 win over Greece in a preliminary game in the men's basketball competition. The game was held at the Helliniko Indoor Arena in Athens during the 2004 Olympic Games on August 17, 2004. Iverson scored 17 points.

bronze medal, Allen showed how much he has matured in the past years. Nobody conducted himself better nor behaved like a better representative than he did in the game. "It's an honor to be named to this team," Iverson said. "This is something that I will cherish even without winning a gold medal," Iverson told reporter Adrian Wojnarowski.

Iverson is as creative off court as he is professionally. He still has a passion for art and draws caricatures and portraits of sports figures. "My art and my basketball go together," he says. "When I draw, I make things up on paper. When I play basketball, I make things up on the court."

CHRONOLOGY

1975 Born in Hampton, Virginia, on June 7.

1993 During senior year in high school, arrested after major brawl at bowling alley. Convicted and serves four months in minimum-security prison. Granted clemency by governor.

1994 Attends Richard Milburn High School in Virginia Beach to earn his last high school credit. Enters Georgetown University. Plays basketball for Coach John Thompson.

1996 Is the smallest first-overall draft pick in NBA history.

1997 Honored as MVP in the Rookie All-Star Game and is Rookie of the Year. Arrested for handgun and marijuana possession, for which he serves 100 hours of community service.

2000 Begins basketball season with controversy over the obscene lyrics in his rap CD that critics claim depict women as objects and make fun of homosexuals. Establishes Crossover Foundation and Allen Iverson Summer Classic Foundation to benefit inner-city youths.

2001 Wins NBA scoring title and league MVP. Leads the Philadelphia 76ers to the NBA Finals. Marries longtime girlfriend Tawanna Turner in August.

2003 Ranks #1 in NBA in steals per game and in minutes played.

2004 For the 50th time, scores 40 points in one game. For the fifth year in a row is named the Eastern Conference All-Star starter. Plays on USA Basketball Men's Senior National team in the 2004 Olympics. Helps team win bronze medal.

2005 Scores 60 points against Orlando Magic, the most in the NBA season. Is named MVP when he helps the East win the NBA All-Star Game for the first time since 2001.

FOR FURTHER READING

Books

Hareas, John. *All-Star Allen Iverson*. Scholastic Paperbacks, 2002.

Mawrence, Amanda. *Allen Iverson*. Triumph Books, 2002.

Platt, Larry. *Only the Strong Survive: The Odyssey of Allen Iverson*. Regan Books, 2002.

Smallwood, John N. *Allen Iverson: Fear No One*. Pocket, 2001.

Stewart, Mark. *Allen Iverson: Motion & Emotion*. Millbrook Press, 2001.

Thornley, Stew. *Allen Iverson: Star Guard (Sports Reports)*. Enslow Publishers, 2001.

Torres, John Albert. *Allen Iverson: Never Give Up (Sports Leaders Series)*. Enslow Publishers, 2004.

Websites

Allen Iverson Chamber
http://iverson.cjb.net
Allen Iverson World
http://www.alleniversonworld.com
Allen Iverson Domain
http://home.c2i.net/espurkel/iverson.htm
ESPN.com: Allen Iverson
http://sports.espn.go.com/nba/players/
profile?statsId=3094
NBA.com
http://www.nba.com/playerfile/allen_iverson

INDEX